# THE LOVING DAD'S HANDBOOK

Raise Them Like Your Life Depends On It

THE LOVING DAD'S HANDBOOK

Raise Them Like Your Life Depends On It

Copyright © 2017 by George Zelina

# THE LOVING DAD'S HANDBOOK

Raise Them Like Your Life Depends On It

GEORGE ZELINA

# INTRODUCTION

**Do you have doubts about how good of a father you are or will be?**
**Are you confused about what it takes to be a loving dad?**

The truth is that every one of us has those moments of doubt, a crisis of confidence or just a nagging worry in the back of our mind, making us unsure of ourselves and the direction to take.

You are about to read a book written by a young father who faced adversity and overcame the problems he faced, with chapters which include:

- **How to develop and master simple techniques to be a good father and partner**
- **How to use these techniques as a part of everyday life**
- **How to overcome fears and doubts**
- **How to become a happier person all around**
- **And much more...**

This book serves as a readable and friendly companion for dads and dads-to-be seeking confidence, guidance, and joy!

# TABLE OF CONTENTS

*Feel free to join my Facebook group (Self-Confidence Boom) for frequent blog posts and motivational quotes as part of this book's offering: https://www.facebook.com/selfconfidenceboom*

# PREFACE

Hi there,

Since we are going to talk about personal things, I hope you will let me use an informal style while talking to you. Thanks.

Fatherhood. I had no idea that it was this complex. I mean, I knew that it would bring changes, but this new chapter of my life is by far the most challenging. And I'm a better man because of it. Being a father is the hardest task, and at the same time the most beautiful experience, a man can face.

I'm a certified life coach, and I believe that parenting and coaching are very much the same, at least in certain aspects. If you want to do it right, you have to be strong, creative, and a good listener. You have to be caring and let your kid experience life in his or her own way, and you have to do this sometimes while standing in the shadows, only acting or reacting if he or she needs you. You have to be a mentor who teaches his child the rules of life, as well as the joys of life, and the values of your family.

I consider this book as a discussion between you and me and not just a book full of practices and how-to tips of parenting. In this book, I will share with you some of my life experience, describe some techniques which have helped me as a father, and ask you different questions which will help you to find your own way as a loving dad.

The first three chapters are getting you prepared for the big day. After that, we will dive deep into the true meaning of being a father. The role model who was there seeing his kid grow up and not the man who looks back and doesn't understand how the whole thing happened in a blink of an eye. Or worse, the man who doesn't look back at all because he just doesn't care.

My father has become the latter, so I have learned how to be a good dad without a decent role model.

One chapter is dedicated solely to an interview with my father. This appeared in my previous book, Self-Confidence Boom, but it has a guaranteed place in this one as well because it truly shows how a father can be responsible for his child's low self-esteem. In this case, mine.

When I saw my little daughter for the first time on a wonderful autumn day, I decided that I would grab the bull by the horns and be the father she deserves. This means that I will be responsible, approachable, and most importantly, available.

Sometimes I will refer to **YouTube videos** and other sources outside of these pages, so I recommend to

1) Use headphones for best experience, if you are reading this book on your smartphone, tablet or computer.
2) Or have your headphones and smartphone/tablet next to you whenever we will watch a video together.

Let's try it out. At the end of this chapter, let me show you a 3-minutes-long YouTube video of an episode from The Fresh Prince of Bel Air starring the young Will Smith. This scene perfectly shows the emotional consequences your kid will face if you just skip this whole fatherhood thing.

**Emotional Dad's Scene from The Fresh Prince of Bel Air**

https://youtu.be/AgkqTFasfmA

*This is a QR code that can be read by e.g.: NeoReader, a smartphone application. This QR code is the same YouTube link you see above.*

I want to be someone like the father... statue at the end of the scene. Every time I shaved, I remembered that I had to learn to shave by myself. There was nobody who would have stood behind me to say, "Don't push the blade so hard, my son, because you will just cut yourself!" We didn't have the chance to talk about my teenage romances or bullying at school. I met with my father once in a week for a couple of hours, but these meetings occurred in computer stores to buy one or two video games. Doom (the original), Prince of Persia (the original) and Wolfenstein (the... Sh.t, I'm getting too old). It had its benefits, but there was a dark side to the story.

I haven't spent quality time with my father. This was one of the catalysts that led to my having extremely and painfully low self-esteem and confidence by the age of 25.

I promised myself that I would do it differently. Ok, so now let's be friends for the next couple of hours.

# FATHERS AND SOON TO BE FATHERS, UNITE

I have faced plenty of challenges throughout my life, from learning to walk, tying my shoelaces, the first day of kindergarten, high school, navigating the social constructs through every stage of life, and a thousand other things besides. I experienced the stress and heartbreak of navigating relationships until I finally met my soulmate and settled down. Then throughout the building of my career as a motivation and self-confidence writer, there were plenty of challenges. It's funny now when I look back and think of all the stress that came from every direction. At the time, it seemed like the worst thing that could ever happen, yet… it came to a point when I realized that it was nothing.

It was nothing compared to the challenges I still had coming. Whenever you think it can't possibly get any more difficult, it does, and if you're convinced it can't, life can't wait to prove you wrong. This is precisely why I decided to write this book, for all the fathers (and soon to be fathers) out there. Because just when you think you have it all worked out, something else crops up.

Parenthood is already a massive challenge, but with society changing the way it has, we face fresh challenges. We are surrounded by the advancement of technology, with social media an ever-present threat, along with smartphones and tablets. Let's face it, fatherhood has changed, and with times changing, so has the concept of fatherhood.

If I really think about it, my parents had it easy. They didn't need to worry about us being cyberbullied, or meeting and dating strangers online. They didn't have to worry about things like embarrassing pictures appearing on the internet, resulting in total humiliation. Parents already had plenty to consider, but with the added complication of technology, we have it much harder than parents of the past.

Sure, we can benefit from the advancements in technology, and handy gadgets that can make life a bit simpler. We can rely on baby monitors that allow us to check up and see our baby resting peacefully (or not) in their nursery, and tools that remind us of the baby's schedule. Do the benefits really outweigh the added pressure? I'm not so sure.

Regardless of the role that technology may play in our lives, we cannot underestimate the role that we, as fathers, play in the lives of our children either. Studies (*references at the end of the book) have shown that the children of confident dads are less likely to experience behavioral problems in their pre-teens. That's right, our attitudes towards fatherhood, from the birth of our children, play a massive part in the development of our kids. Our emotional response, and our emotional connection to parenthood have a serious effect on our children.

All this time we've been busy with throwing babies in the air, stacking cheerios on their foreheads, chasing, tickling, and making them laugh, only to find out that child development has a lot to do with us! We've always assumed that mothers play the most important role in the development of the children because, traditionally speaking, mothers do most of the caring. So, the focus has always been on the mental health of mothers, and their parenting skills.

The emotional impact of a father on his children has been long overlooked, to our children's detriment. We have a duty to be heavily involved with the development of our children from the time they are born. We need to be confident in our ability to raise children and engaged with our children emotionally. This flies in the face of everything we've ever been told about parenting! Remember, when you were young and TV dads were always there to enforce rules, while being grumpy the rest of the time? Every once in a while, there would be a storyline and dad would slip his arm around his kid and share an almost emotional moment? That was it. That was as close as our favorite TV sitcom dads came to expressing an emotional competence and confidence.

I don't know how you were raised, but most of us fathers-to-be were raised believing it isn't okay to cry or to be in touch with your emotions. I'm not suggesting you need to cry, or that you need to be overtly emotional. Though, if you are, that's cool. There's nothing wrong with that. There is absolutely nothing wrong with being in touch with your emotions. I remember crying through the whole cast list of Titanic in the cinema. Poor Leo. As the study above bears out, our emotions have a serious impact on our children.

How big an impact? How about this:

- **33%** - When biological fathers are highly involved in their children's upbringing, the children are 33% less likely to repeat a grade. (U.S. Dept. of Education study, Nord, C., & West, J. 2001)
- **43%** - When children's biological fathers are highly involved, they are 43% more likely to achieve mostly A's. (U.S. Dept. of Education study, Nord, C., & West, J. 2001)

- **85%** - The percentage of youth exhibiting behavioral disorders... come from a fatherless home. (Urban Leadership Institute's Dare to Be King, 2006)
- **90%** - This is the percentage of runaway and homeless youth that are the result of a fatherless home. (Urban Leadership Institute's Dare to Be King, 2006)
- **0%** - This is the percentage of chance to restart the levels you will finish in the video game called '*Your Kid's Childhood.*'

Sorry, I know, I'm probably freaking you out. If you're a new dad or a soon to be father, you're probably already nervous enough about raising children. Hey, moms feel a lot of pressure to be the best, so it's only fair that we share some of that burden. There's a lot to take in when you find out you're going to be a dad, but let's not forget that moms also have a lot to deal with like, you know, baking that bun that you helped make for almost a year.

# I Will Be a Dad

It's truly incredible when you think about it, how your life can change in just one day, in just a couple of minutes really. Yet, the day the pregnancy test comes back positive is the day your entire world will not only turn upside down, but be shaken vigorously until everything comes loose. I remember pouring out a long shot of Whisky and puffing a Cuban cigar in just a few minutes right after I saw that beautiful + sign.

You are now faced with preparing for an entirely new and totally different life. I'm going to make this as clear as I can for you: you're going to mess up, a lot. If that wasn't bad enough, you're going to be messing up for the foreseeable future.

New parents are embarking on a new path; it's a journey where you'll only learn from mistakes if you make them. Luckily, it's going to happen. If you choose to have more kids, you'll find yourself correcting initial mistakes. With baby number 1, you may find yourself being super protective, and maybe even a tad overbearing. Don't worry, you'll get tired of that.

You may be rolling your eyes, thinking that nothing *really* changes when parenthood comes knocking on your door. Can you hear that? That's the laughter of all the parents who have come before you. The truth is, *everything* changes, instantly. Every first-time father will soon learn all the experiences from those who blazed the trail before them. From those who are desperate to tell you it's the best thing that will ever happen to you, and those that will regale you with stories about how they haven't slept in 7 years. If you're really lucky, you'll know a dad who has dealt with a colicky baby – like me.

Then there are the *other* dads, those dads that will look at you smugly, with blatant pity, a look that says you don't know what's coming. Guess what? You really don't know what's coming. You can do your best to prepare, but how can you prepare for something you have never experienced? Even if you grew up in with a multitude of siblings, it isn't quite the same as bringing your own child into the world. Perhaps the best advice that can be offered to any man dealing with impending fatherhood is: expect everything to change instantly.

For all this time, it's just been you and your lady, and now there's something between you: your baby. That's a terrible way to put it, but it's the truth. When this baby arrives, you aren't each other's everything anymore. Expect to feel a little sidelined, because your sole focus will be on your brand-new baby. Some guys get jealous, but you don't need to, because this is your baby, too. Expect your partner to pour her undivided attention onto the baby, which can be exhausting for her. So, make sure that rather than getting jealous, you give her extra attention, and help her take care of the baby when it arrives.

In the meantime, there will be plenty to plan and handle. You'll be shopping for all the necessary supplies, including swing chairs, changing tables, crib, nursery accessories and décor, strollers, and more. Your baby will take over your life before it even arrives. You may not be interested in these things, but the least you can do is pretend to be interested, and try to help with the process. Pregnancy is exhausting, so your wife will need you to stay strong, even if you're bored out of your mind. Not to mention, there are plenty of things you need to take care of in the run up to the baby arriving.

Before the baby arrives, you'll need to take care of:

- **The crib.** Now, no one is suggesting that you whittle your own wood here. However, no matter what crib you settle on, it takes time to put it all together. Don't leave it till the last minute; it's a project that is fun, quick, and easy. Maybe you can crack open a beer and listen to music while handling a giant puzzle.

**Watch Ryan Reynolds Trying to Build an IKEA Crib**
https://youtu.be/-wXjs6DXoeY

*This is a QR code that can be read by e.g.: NeoReader, a smartphone application. This QR code is the same YouTube link you see above.*

- **The car seat.** This is a must, so it needs to be taken care of in advance so that you can get your baby home safely. In fact, some hospitals won't release a baby until they have checked the vehicle to ensure there is a car seat installed correctly. When it comes to newborns, you will need a combination of baby carrier and car seat. You'll need to install the base of the car seat in the car. Ensure that you follow the instruction manual to install the car seat properly. It's important to make sure you get this done right, so take your time - after all, it is an issue of safety. The good news is that you have your work checked. Many fire departments have a safety seat program. You can swing by the station with the car and have them check to ensure it's correctly installed. No, they won't let you play on the fire poles. Me and my silly bucket list.

- **The nursery.** You'll want to get the nursery completed in plenty of time, in case baby arrives early. You may have painting and decorating to do, or some picture and decoration hanging to handle. Regardless of the task, make sure you smile and take care of it when your wife asks.

- **Honey do list.** Most couples have a list of tasks that need to get done, and most often they're ignored. If you have a baby on the way, though, it's probably a good time to put a dent in that list. You won't have time to fix things around the house once the baby arrives, and you don't want a toddler exposing all your flaws. Take this opportunity to get things ready for the new arrival. Including any baby-proofing that you may need to take care of.

# WHAT'S GOING ON WITH HER?

Now that your soulmate is pregnant, your life will change. The next 9 months aren't just about her carrying the baby while your life continues as scheduled. Certain things are expected of you, and there are particular things that you can do to make her life easier.

Here's the thing. She has the responsibility of carrying your child, of making smart decisions that will fuel the development of your children in utero, as well as sacrificing things that she loves for the good of your child. She has to say goodbye to alcohol, while you can still enjoy a brew or two. She can forget sushi, and to be honest - a lot of seafood, plus she can forget enjoying a rare steak. Deli meat is out, and so are soft cheeses, raw eggs, pate, and caffeine. That's just what she can't eat! She can also kiss goodbye to bungee jumping and skydiving, total bummer.

She will be overwhelmed with hormones, and emotions that she cannot control. The majority of the time she will handle this like a total champ. Unfortunately, there will be times when it becomes too much. In these cases, it's up to you to offer support, comfort, and a shoulder to cry on. You.are.her.safety.net.

You may find the process bewildering, struggling with what to do, and in some cases a lot of dads back away, rather than stepping up. Don't worry, I've got your back! Here are just a few of the ways you can take care of your love.

First of all, if this is an unplanned pregnancy, don't respond negatively. Inappropriate responses include: tears of rage, a face of disgust, and throwing accusations. You want her to believe that you're capable of being a great dad, so responding like a child isn't going to fill her with confidence.

It's time to start reading up on pregnancy. It's important that you take time to read about what she'll be going through. This will make it a lot easier for you to empathize with her, and understand what it is she's going through. There are plenty of books out there to choose from, and many of them are aimed at dads (like this one!). It just makes sense to understand what she will expect during every stage of the pregnancy.

The 3$^{rd}$ thing serves a three-pronged approach. Make time to attend all of her doctor's appointments. The first thing it shows her is that you are in this completely, and you've got her back. The second is that you'll know what is happening in the pregnancy, making you far more prepared to help. Listen to what the doctor says at the appointments, because she may be excited and nervous at these appointments, and pregnant women do have memory blips. The third is all about seeing your baby on screen and hearing that little heartbeat. Your bond starts there. I remember continuously smiling on the way back home while hearing only one thing: Bam-bam-bam-bam... 140 bpm.

It's equally important to help reduce her stress levels, and help her with sleep. Pregnancy is demanding, both emotionally and physically. Don't place a burden on her that isn't necessary, and do your best to pick up extra chores so that she can rest. While you're snoring, she will be struggling with comfort and unable to sleep, especially the later, it is in the pregnancy. If she sleeps on her back, then the baby will be applying pressure to the spine, intestines, back muscles, and all of the major blood vessels. This is painful, and makes for a difficult night's sleep.

Here are a few tips which may help your pregnant lady get some sleep.

- A full body pillow can make side sleeping much more comfortable. Don't forget to try it out yourself. I'm still using it during Siestas over the weekends.

- Herbal teas relax both the body and the mind. Even if she hesitated, be the man and go to the kitchen! *Wait, what?!* Just make her a cup of tea.

- Give her a back massage just before bed. When we got to know each other, one of my pick-up lines was that I'm a certified Shiatsu masseur. After a couple of months, I told her that it was a 2-days-long training and half of the time other participants gave me massages. I'm simply a natural. Anyway, it helps her relax and rejuvenate.

- Make time for cuddles. She is still your woman, and she needs a man to protect her and your baby.

Patience is a virtue, and you need it because pregnancy is going to wreak havoc. She may feel great one day, and the next day experience a total breakdown, where she can't stop the tears. Be patient, and know that it's hormones. Her sex drive will also change, it's usually gone during the first 3 months, back with a vengeance for the next 3, and then dips again in those last 3. It's all about understanding and patience.

With all the changes her body is going through, you need to take time to let her know that you love her and that she is beautiful. Tell her she's beautiful every single day. It's not that hard. If you read my previous book, Self-Confidence Boom, you're already doing it for yourself. Extend the VIP list of 1 with your soulmate.

Around 75% of pregnant women are hit with serious morning sickness, and it hits after the first month. It usually disappears after 14 weeks or so, but this is the thing: it doesn't just happen in the morning. It usually lasts all day, and some remedies can help her get through.

- **Crackers** – She won't be able to eat much; an empty stomach is going to make things a lot worse. Crackers can help prevent nausea, and they're easy on her stomach.
- **Supplements** – Specifically vitamin B6, which helps to alleviate symptoms. In addition, magnesium relaxes muscles, while calcium stimulates muscles to contract.
- **Ginger ale** – Or any clear soda. The fizziness will help fight nausea.
- **Peppermint tea** – Or ginger tea, can decrease the feelings of nausea.
- **Stay clean** – When women are pregnant, they're incredibly sensitive to smells. Make sure you shower every day, that you're brushing your teeth, and prepare to sideline your aftershave.
- **Be flexible** – Understand that your wife may want one food desperately one day, and not be able to stomach it the next. Get her whatever it is she wants, even if it means running to the store.
- **Seasickness bracelets** – It's just an elastic band that has plastic

bumps which apply pressure to various points of the wrist. This can give her some relief.

You have to understand that pregnancy can be freakin' scary. You need to be prepared to let your wife cry, vent, or whatever, at any time of the day. If she's worried about something specifically, then do some research so that you can set her mind at ease.

# THE DAY OF THE BIRTH

You've spent the last 9 months providing support and making preparations, and now the big day has finally arrived. Are you ready?

Throughout the history of humankind, baby delivery has been an activity deemed women's work. Dad would stay outside the room, or in the waiting room, and pace while waiting for news of the arrival. His chief responsibility was to announce the birth, and hand out cigars (bubblegum or real) and exclaim the gender excitedly.

Now, though, the majority of couples opt for the father to be in the room, right by mom's side throughout the entire process. I remember the doctor was drawing bunnies on my wife's back to entertain us during the "boring" parts. There may be people who don't love the idea of this, but there is nothing like seeing your child make its entrance into the world. You can't imagine the emotions I felt as my daughter took her first breaths and let out a scream.

More important, though, how can you support your wife as she gives birth to your child?

The first step is to have the "go" bag ready. When it's time for the big arrival, you don't want to be running around shoving random items in a bag. So, have a bag packed and ready to go. Make sure the following items are in the bag:

- **Snacks.** You might be thinking that snacks don't belong on this list, let alone at the top. The truth of the matter is that lots of dads forget to eat in all the excitement, which often results in fainting during childbirth. Your friends will laugh at you because you couldn't handle a bit of blood or goo, but the truth is: it's all down to a failure to eat. Bring handy snacks and drinks. And then you won't need to worry about sneaking away for sustenance.

- **Sweatshirt.** It can be a bit chilly in hospitals, and probably you will be pretty tired, so no matter what time of year it is, you should have a long-sleeved shirt, hoodie, or sweatshirt handy.

- **Toiletries.** Not just toiletries, though, but also a change of clothes. Once the baby has arrived, your wife and baby may stay for a day or two. So, it's important that you have a change of clothes, and a toothbrush, at the very least. Don't forget the new baby's outfit!

- **Camera.** You want to capture the memories of a lifetime on (digital) film. You want to take pictures of the process, and of the new baby.

- **Entertainment.** Childbirth can be a long and tedious process. If your wife opts for an epidural, then she'll be in and out of sleep, and you'll be at wit's end. So, make sure you have a book, magazines, or a device that will keep you entertained for hours on end (don't forget chargers). I remember replaying Uncharted for the third time on my PS Vita.

The support you provide her during the birth is important. You are her coach and her support as she goes through a seriously nerve-racking process. Think of your role as encompassing the following:

- **The hand holder.** If you're planning on having an epidural, then the birth isn't going to look much like the sweat covered lady, panting and screaming that we've become so used to seeing on the big screen. In the case of an epidural, there isn't a whole lot for you to do, besides holding her hand and helping her through. Your job will be: the rock. You are the calm and confident guy, who is there to offer a reassuring word, look, and even tell a joke or two when the moment is right. You also need to be prepared to be flexible, because not every birth runs smoothly. No matter what happens, stay level-headed.

- **The leg holder.** There's nothing fancy or glamorous about this job, but be prepared to hold your wife's legs. The doctor may ask you to help out when it comes time to push. Let the doctor call the shots and direct your wife when to push, do as you're told, and be the cheerleader she needs. If you are a leg holder, you'll get an excellent view of your baby crowning. This is an incredible experience, and it will stay with you forever. Don't think about it as gross, or feel repulsed by life coming from your favorite spot… that's weird. This is life, and while it may seem crazy, it's cool.

- **The interference runner.** Every mom has a different personality, so the role here will differ. Some moms create birth plans that specify what types of medications will be involved, and how the birth should unfold. If you have one of these "birth plans," then you need to make the medical staff aware of it. It's your job to run interference between them and your wife. Don't get in the way, but ask what's happening when they're getting ready to do something. Make sure that whatever they suggest is necessary medically, and if it isn't, then ask them to follow your birth plan.

Your wife isn't going to be able to handle everything, so be the guy that stays on top of it all. Be the project manager who is a good communicator, always available, and who focuses on the important stuff.

- **The cutter of the cord.** It will very likely fall into your hands to cut the cord, thus giving your baby its freedom. Well, not total freedom. It will be quite some time before the "apron strings" are cut.

This role will look different for everyone, and some may handle it better than others. For the most part, it will depend on your personality type. The important thing to remember is that it's your job to be the rock your wife can rely on. Handle things as they crop up. Just think of it as an extension of the support that you've been providing throughout the pregnancy, concentrated in one epic culmination. Nothing can prepare you for the flood of emotions that you will feel when you hold your baby for the first time. P-R-I-C-E-L-E-S-S!

# LET'S GET THE PARTY STARTED

Your baby has *finally* arrived, the wait is over, and it's time to get started.

First things first, when the baby first arrives, you should expect a fairly wrinkly, sticky, gooey, cone-shaped mess. Don't worry; the baby will normalize after a few days (or weeks).

The breastfeeding. Not every mom chooses to breastfeed, but if your wife does, then this generally starts within an hour after the birth. Make sure you keep visitors at bay to allow your wife a bit of calm for this first feed. You can either hold off on calling your family or ask them to wait a bit before visiting. Whatever you're most comfortable with. While breastfeeding may be the most natural thing, it doesn't always come easy. Sex is natural, but just think about the first time you did it... it wasn't smooth sailing, was it? It can be difficult, and it is extremely stressful when you get started. You'd be surprised how much help you can be in helping your wife get the right position so that the baby can latch on to eat.

Be prepared to change a lot of diapers because your wife is going to be exhausted in the days following birth. In fact, in some ancient cultures, women were to spend *months* in bed after giving birth. The expectation was for the family to step up and do all the dirty work and deliver the baby for feeding and cuddles. A lot has changed since then!

You'll also get a lot of visitors in the weeks following a birth, so make sure you take control of this. Be prepared to shoo away certain visitors who are overstaying their welcome, or to turn them away if your wife isn't up to it. Grandparents and relatives can be overwhelming when you are trying to get used to your new lives. Forget feelings, your top priorities are mother and baby.

You've probably heard that babies use a lot of diapers. Well, the rumor is true. You should start a diaper collection as soon as you find out that your wife is pregnant. Look out for deals and pick up plenty in advance. You will thank me later.

Now that your baby has arrived, you're probably going to be exhausted. Sleeping in will be a thing of the past, while unbroken sleep is the new norm. There are ways to get through, though, I promise.

- **Nap when you can.** If you can fit in a nap somewhere between your father duties and your job, then do it. It will make a world of difference to your life. On weekends, you can take turns getting up so that you can each catch a few extra winks. Saturday could be your day, and Sunday could be hers. Introducing appointed nap times was a game changer for us. After several weeks of insomnia, we decided that I would be on duty for two nights in a row. My wife only came in to breastfeed. The first night was catastrophic. Both the baby and I were mostly awake all night long. But on the next night, she slept for 5 hours in a row. It was a miracle in those desperate times. After that, the nights were smooth for months, until a new tooth wanted to come out.

- **Activity.** You need to stay active, but so does the baby. Try to keep your baby active and alert throughout the day so that they're all tuckered out for bed in the evening.

- **Diet.** Your diet is what is going to fuel you through your days. Make sure you eat a hearty breakfast, and if you want to avoid a mid-morning slump, avoid coffee. Make sure you drink plenty of water because hydration is crucial. Make sure you pack a lunch for work. It should include some almonds and fruit to keep you fueled throughout your afternoon. This will put you in good stead to handle whatever the baby can throw at you when you get home from work.

- **Preparation.** Kids are stressful, and you can help mom out by getting everything ready for her the night before. It will improve her quality of sleep and yours, too.

- **Pick me ups.** As delicious as coffee is, peppermint tea is a great way to perk things up.

The most important thing is to overcome the tiredness that is dragging both of you down so that you can enjoy this new life that you have brought into the world. Don't be afraid to accept help, and if someone offers to watch the baby to allow you to enjoy adult time together, then accept it. If you spend all of your time looking after a baby, you'll forget what it's like to be around adults. Hanging out with other grownups is important for your sanity. The truth is, there were times when I felt like I was the main actor in Falling Down 2. I picked up my phone and called my best friend to meet ASAP. That helped a lot.

It's also important to look after mom. She'll have her own medical care and checkups to attend, including the postpartum checkup. It's important that you encourage your wife to be open and honest about her experience. If she's overly tired, she should say so, because the doctor may want to do some checks. There are medical issues that crop up after a new baby arrives, and these can make mom more tired. She also has emotional needs, so pay attention to how she's feeling. If she's feeling depressed, or a bit blue, get her to open up and talk to you about it. She should also tell her doctor. Many women struggle with postpartum depression, and it can be treated.

Make sure that you spend time as a family. Wrap baby up and head out to enjoy the outdoors together. It gets all of you out of the house, to prevent you from going stir crazy, and allows you to spend time with each other, as well as enjoy the baby.

As your child gets a little older, consider preschool. You may not *need* preschool, but it can be good for the child and for mom. It allows mom some time to engage in adult things, rest, and recharge. It also offers your child a chance to socialize from a young age, especially if it's your first child.

Don't be afraid to switch roles either. If you feel more inclined to caring for the children, then don't be afraid to be a house husband, while your wife goes out to work. It's all about making the right choices for *your* family.

Enjoying this book so far? I'd love for you to share your thoughts and post a quick review on Amazon!

# Family Bonds

Five years ago, I was battling with excess weight, and my self-confidence was equal to zero. Every time I looked in the mirror I had a specific scene from the movie 'The Last Boy Scout' running in my mind where Bruce Willis is talking to himself staring in the rear-view mirror: "Nobody likes you. Everybody hates you. You're gonna lose. Smile you fuck." Then I smiled pathetically at the mirror and continued my daily routine without any pleasure, knowing that nothing will change because everyone is against me and what is more, I have to share my body with my biggest enemy – myself.

**The scene from 'The Last Boy Scout'**
https://youtu.be/5ChZN8SDbwo

*This is a QR code that can be read by e.g.: NeoReader, a smartphone application. This QR code is the same YouTube link you see above.*

To regain my self-confidence, an important milestone was to understand my own father's motives and decisions as a parent. That is why I asked him to have an interview with me.

It was a bright summer day, the day of the interview and the naked truth.

After I had arrived at my dad's place, I laid down on the couch without asking anything. Dad could see that I was tired so he started making some coffee without asking anything. Holding a tape-recorder in his hand, he sat down on an armchair next to the couch and by spinning his glasses in his hands, he started the conversation.

- Do you ever talk to your friends about what relationship they have with their fathers?
- Rarely.
- Rarely? Why?
- For many people, it is a very sensitive subject. It is so intimate that you can't just talk about it during an everyday chat.
- So, what happens is that a child is born and the mother and the father are busy with how much food the baby has eaten, what the neighbours said about him, how granny picked him up, and they call each other every hour so that they can capture every moment. Then there is the graduation causing a lot of stress for the family. After that, the parents have almost no clue what's going on with their child until their grandchild is born. Based on your age, I guess you can't really tell me why it's like that – do you have any idea?
- I have some ideas, but I would like to give you the chance to answer this question.
- The child and their parents don't talk that much after a certain age, though I am sure you had a lot more going on in your life after graduation than before that. Have you missed chatting with me?

- Yes, I have.

- Then why didn't you call me? Why didn't we talk?

At that moment, that good old mocha pot started giving a high pitch noise signalling that the coffee was ready. We walked to the kitchen and made our coffees the way we both like: with a little bit of milk and no sugar.

We went back and sat down where we had been sitting. Our coffees were steaming on the coffee table, and he asked me the same questions again:

- Why didn't you call me if you missed talking with me? Why didn't we talk?

- The teenager pride and the illusion of independence eventually turned into a routine so that I could solve my own problems alone or with the help of friends and I didn't need parental advice.

- Do you think it's the same in every child-parent relationship?

- I think mostly it is, but I dare to say that our relationship is much better than the average. You know about my everyday life.

- Do you know what's wrong with what you're saying? You think that I know about your things. I know very little. I know where you work. I know who you are because I can sense you. We go and talk to our friends. We talk about women, football, what hurts, what movie we have seen with our friends. We laugh, we complain, but I can't see the same between a father and his son. Although, do you agree that we get on well?

- Yes, I do.

- Then why is it so?
- I think we live very much in the present and we share our current things with people who we get in touch with daily. What I mean is that I don't spend just a "How're you doing?" chit chat time with my friends, but we can usually spend more time together.
- Do you want to know why I didn't let myself down after breaking up my 20-year-old marriage?
- Because of us?
- Then why did I leave you 20 years ago?
- You didn't leave us. We have constantly been in touch. You didn't wriggle out of your fatherly duties - in fact, you managed to prove that it is not necessarily a split family if the father lives separately.
- You were 8 years old when your mom and I got divorced. I decided that I wasn't going to watch a single cartoon until you turn 18. I wasn't going to touch any books for children, and I was not going to look after any children. I used to talk to you in my imagination through the night. I went through hell. I think I must share the mistakes I have made with you. I have noticed that generation after generation make the same mistakes. They just don't learn from their parents' examples. It is because they don't talk honestly about their problems. There is an example that happened in front of my eyes. There was a man who had a son. The man used to say that he had a headache at the most inappropriate times. During lunchtime, at the interval of a football match, during shopping or walking. His son grew up constantly complaining about headaches as well, although it turned out later that it was psychosomatic. Not hearing anything

else, it was ingrained into his mind. He learned it just the way he learned to walk and speak. So, you were saying you had very low self-esteem? How did you get there?

- I considered my failures bigger than my success in every area of my life. While disappointments poisoned my thoughts, success made a little smile flicker around my lips and then I quickly forgot about it.

- I should have sensed that you were going through a bad patch.

- It's my fault too that you didn't sense it. I didn't put you in the picture. For some reason, I chose to become a family member whose duty it was to listen to everyone and to solve their inner conflicts. I didn't want the family to know about my personal problems.

- You didn't like yourself at that time, did you? You were dissatisfied with yourself, weren't you?

- I didn't like myself.

- Why not?

- Let's start with my appearance. I always found something to disapprove of in myself. My big double chin, those big bags under my eyes, my trousers being too tight. I could continue this all-day long. I was discontented all the time. On the other hand, I constantly felt that I couldn't function well in a relationship. I felt that if I had hooked up with someone, I wouldn't find my way. Before even getting there with someone, I was already thinking about what I would screw up.

- This is my responsibility. An 8-year-old boy went through all this because of his dad, and it even had an impact on his youth.

- You can't say that it's your responsibility.

- If we just make things look better to ourselves, we just hush them up. I want to emphasize that a child is a lot bigger responsibility than someone's private life. Do you realize what consequences this has? 10, 15, 20 years go by, and a clever, intelligent young man is about to have a budding relationship without self-esteem and without being able to square his shoulders. Son, there is no divorce without the parents and their children getting hurt. 19 years have gone by, and the wound hasn't healed, in fact, it has been contaminated. How can we solve it? Do you believe that your soul and your body are synchronized and that your soul's language is illness?

- Yes, completely.

- I know that you suffer from high blood pressure, especially under stress. What was the last stressful situation in your life?

- Exactly a year ago, I had to stand in front of 150 people and gave them a presentation in my second language about a job-related topic. Before that, I had been uptight for days and weeks rehearsing the speech in front of the mirror and with friends too. Then, when they called me to go to the stage, and I started walking, the world around me slowed down, I started to hear my heart beating, I began to sweat, and each of my steps felt like a hammer hitting my eardrums. It was a terrible feeling. I did the presentation but I was feeling very uncomfortable, and I couldn't wait to finish and get off the stage.

- Let's play a game. Imagine that you are there again. They are calling you but not just you, they are calling me as well. I start the speech: "I'm here because I am proud of my son. I am standing on this stage so that you can see that I am his father. Son, do the presentation. Please, don't applaud me."

Here we had a break - I am not ashamed to confess that I burst into tears. A feeling deep inside me was freed, a feeling that I didn't know had been suppressed. It was such a relief!

- Let me tell you about the latest stressful adventure I had. After my leg surgery, I was told that I might need to spend the rest of my life in a wheelchair. I was astonished and shocked by this news. I was staring into space for minutes. 10 minutes later you came to the hospital, and I forgot what I had been told. I wondered if you were in a similar situation one day, what you would need to do. Half a year later, I was jogging on Margaret Island in Budapest. Do you believe in self-healing?
- Yes, I do. The soul can be healed.
- Self-healing kick-starts a process, but the family should join it. You can heal a lot, but without your family, it's impossible to recover completely. For example, I need you for my recovery.
- I think what we are talking about now is too specific. There might be a lot of people who don't have the opportunity to involve their family in their healing. A lot of families are not open to help each other on this level.
- One of the cornerstones in the way to heal ourselves is to clear our minds. We must be honest and say what bothers us, what hurts us. Even if our family doesn't support us in it. If someone gets to this point, they should look at what they have been doing wrong, and their family must help them. It's a must!
- Let's have a look at the following example. There is a boy, and his father is an alcoholic. How will he ask his father to talk to him?
- Do you know why he became an alcoholic?
- No.

- Neither do they, because they never talk about it. They don't sit down to talk when he is sober. They don't start healing each other. They don't have to talk about what we are talking about now – they must do what we are doing. Help each other and themselves.
- If none of them are open, it doesn't work.
- You should knock on this door until it opens. It is a bond forever. It's impossible to tear it apart.
- Suppose one of them dies.
- People can talk to their family members without being physically in the same space at the same time. I am still talking with my mother who passed on 40 years ago. Let's move on! Do you believe that if you write down the things you want to achieve on a piece of paper and keep it close by all the time, it will help?
- Yes. From time to time I write down all the things I want to achieve and put this little piece of paper into a little box on the shelf where I can see it occasionally. Whenever that list comes to my mind, I open the box and go through the list. If something is obsolete, I cross that one out. If there is something I wish for but not on the list, I just add it as a new one. It's interesting to see how my wishes change month by month, year by year.
- What does your paper say?
- It doesn't say that I want to be the CEO of Google. It has healthy goals on it. A life without mortgage in X years' time...
- Go on!
- ... A stable financial background and a happy family in 5 years involving you too, as a grandparent.
- Are you a forgiving type of person?

- Yes, I am.

- What does forgiveness mean?

- It means that you get over the pains caused by someone else, reflect on it, and forgive them.

- Have you forgiven me for leaving you?

- You didn't leave us, but yes, I have no resentment.

- Do you want to know what forgiveness means to me? The same thing you have just said but there is another type of forgiveness, the one when you should forgive yourself. You are not angry with me, but I am upset with myself.

- Why?

- Because you had to stand in front of 150 people hearing your own heartbeat, because you suffered from obesity, because you set goals at the age of 27 that you can easily reach. You know, revealing the truth is important. If you take the responsibility to help other people, you must clean your wounds. That is the message of this conversation.

- Are you saying that all my issues can be traced back to you?

- Yes, that's what I am saying. We are skating on thin ice, and I am balancing on a knife edge. If you haven't thought about it, well, here comes the real part of forgiveness. You either get better or your wound gets even worse, but you must take this risk. Everyone should take the risk.

- What would you write on your paper?

- Let all your obstacles come down! When you were 8 you could open my fridge any time you wanted. Now I want you to open it any time you want. If you need my shoes, take them. If you need my phone, take it. If you want to live here, live here. You have a house because I have a house. You will find your other half because you are lovable. Your life will be so stable that nobody will want to leave you. You will have children because they will come when everything works out fine. You will have everything you want.

Before talking to my dad, I hadn't realized that my relationship with my dad could have played a role in my low self-esteem. All I felt sometimes was a gap in our father-son relationship.

# A CONFIDENT CHILD

We often underestimate what type of confidence it truly takes to be a kid. Just think about how nerve racking it was for you to go to a new school, or to step up to the plate for the first time. Our kids face uncharted territory all the time, and it's easy to forget that by getting caught up in our own stuff.

It's natural for parents to want to instill a good attitude in kids, providing them with confidence to face every new challenge the same - with self-belief. Every child is different, but there are plenty of ways to build their confidence and ensure they feel loved.

Self-confidence comes from competence. Your children won't be confident because you tell them they're amazing, but because of their accomplishments, whether big or small. Encouraging words are great, but they mean more when they match an ability or achievement. I'm talking about the Nobel Peace Prize, either. When a baby learns to clap their hands, that's a big deal, so you make a big deal out of it. The same goes when they learn how to crawl, walk, brush their teeth, dress themselves, tie their shoelaces, ride a bike, make the bed, and so on. These milestones make kids feel capable.

Every milestone comes with an increase in confidence. You can help your kids by providing them with plenty of opportunities to practice, allowing them to make mistakes, and encouraging them to get back up and try again. When your children show you a new skill, react with excitement, praise their achievements.

By instructing them well from birth through the little accomplishments, you are setting them up for success when they face bigger challenges. Your children can tackle anything with confidence because they've been successful in a variety of other areas.

Consider these tips to raising confident children:

- **Don't control, coach.** It's up to kids to do, and to play the game, whereas coaches assist in developing skills. As a parent, you're the coach; we just support the kids and provide them with the opportunity to develop, and flourish. It's not about doing it *for* your kids, but allowing them to *do*. Do things *with* your kids, show them the way, and then let them do it for themselves.

- **The goal isn't perfection.** Every parent faces the temptation of wanting to improve something their child has done. Constantly interfering and intervening will only serve to undermine your child's confidence, it will also prevent them from learning things for themselves.

- **Let them try for themselves.** You're not abandoning your kids if you allow them to try things themselves as early as possible. It's easier than you think, simply stand aside and let your kids go. You'll be standing nearby, ready to offer encouragement, or help if it's really necessary.

- **Tackle manageable challenges.** This is known as scaffolding, because you're essentially providing your child with a framework to build on. You can do this by demonstrating something, or explaining it to them, and then allow them to carry it out. Each successful attempt at these small challenges will build confidence and encourage them to try new things. It's also important for your children to know they can turn to you when they need help, especially before they get to those hormonal years.

- **Don't set your kids up for failure.** You should provide your kids with a structure to succeed. If you see failure ahead, do you allow your child to learn the lesson, or should you step in and help? It's difficult because by rescuing your kids, it can stop them from learning difficult and important lessons. Then again, kids can feel unloved if their parents allow them to fail. They don't learn the necessary lesson, they instead feel like the failure, and struggle with future failure. Is stepping in rescuing them? Well, that depends on how you do it. If you take control over a science project only to do the majority of it the night before it's due, that's not rescuing. That's just showing your kids that you'll bail them out if he or she fails to put in the necessary work. However, if you help at every stage, resisting the urge to take over, then your child will complete the task, and you both have something to be proud of.

- **Encourage.** We all need encouragement. Not only will encouraging your kids make them feel motivated and positive, but it will instill an inner voice that will continue to encourage them throughout life. Come up with helpful mantras. Shared wisdom and words of encouragement help us manage our frustration. So, when your son fails to pass his test for a brown belt, or your daughter makes a mistake during a violin recital, they'll have that comforting voice driving them. **Empathize and describe.** If you tell your child they did a good job, you're not providing them with adequate information about what it was they did well. Learn to be descriptive in your praise, and empathize adequately with the emotions that they're experiencing at the moment.

- **Effort, not results.** You should always offer positive feedback to your kids about specific things they have control over. For instance, emphasize perseverance and hard work, rather than intelligence, which they have no control over. The point isn't the product, but the effort. You don't want your child to rest on their laurels, whether they're four or fifteen. Your goal is for your child to always try and keep practicing, to get better, and to learn that goals can be accomplished through hard work.

- **Don't be afraid of feelings.** Your child will deal with frustration, and when they do, your empathy is critical. It isn't about removing the source of frustration, rather it's about creating a context through communication. Offer compassion about the circumstance that your child is encountering. It's natural for children to feel frustrated, and to experience disappointment. Your child may sulk or even cry all day long, but offering your child unconditional understanding will help the grieving process. When your child has overcome this, they'll be able to try again next time. This is how our kids develop resilience.

It is also very important to avoid comparison of your child to other children, your partner or yourself. If you have to compare, ask an expert and don't speculate or google all-day-long for an answer.

*"Does she grow as fast as little Billy?"*
*"Is he running as fast as Jude?"*

*"Why is she a worse athlete than I was at her age?"*

*"Why does Julie get higher grades at school than my son?"*

All of us are different. If you accept this basic fact, all of your lives will be easier because your child won't grow up in a competitive environment.

# Baby Blues

You probably didn't realize that around 8 in 10 women end up with the baby blues in the first few weeks following birth. And 10% of new moms experience postpartum depression. Once the baby arrives, both parents have all new roles in life, and settling into these new roles can be frustrating.

It can be terrifying to watch your partner deal with baby blues (or postpartum depression). You'll want to make her feel better, but you won't really know how.

Now, if you know the symptoms to look out for, then you'll have a better idea of how to proceed.

The baby blues strikes within just a few days of birth and generally lasts just a few weeks. The symptoms of baby blues include:

- Loss of appetite.
- Mood swings.
- Irritability.
- Crying spells.

Postpartum depression, by contrast, can occur in the weeks following birth and last up to a year following it. Many of the baby blues symptoms are also present in postpartum depression, but they are much more intense, and they last longer. The additional symptoms of postpartum depression are:

- Anxiety.

- Severe depression.

- Insomnia.

- Extreme fatigue.

- Isolating herself from social and/or physical contact.

- Feelings of hopelessness, or being overwhelmed.

- An irrational alarm over the baby, or a lack of interest in it.

If you think that your partner may be experiencing this, you'll need to seek professional help. You can't wait for the symptoms to get worse, or even for her to ask for help, it's important for her to get help immediately. If you do notice these signs, then talk to her. Talk to her about how and what she is going through and feeling.

New parenthood is difficult enough, but living with someone who is handling depression is incredibly frustrating. You can't fix this; only a professional can help.

The following tips may also be of use:
- Depression improves with consistent support from a partner.

- Recovery will take longer, the longer you ignore the issue or pretend it isn't happening.

- Recovery will be more difficult if you continue to place demands on her.

- Being hard on yourself won't help, it will simply drain your energy.

- Things will get better.

Now, your partner may not be handling baby blues or postpartum depression, but that doesn't mean she may not feel low from time to time.

When you're dealing with mood swings, it may be difficult to communicate.

- You may tell her you love her, yet she doesn't believe you.
- You may text to let her know you're stuck working late, but she'll believe it's because you don't want to come home to her and the baby.
- You may tell her she's gorgeous, and she'll think you're lying.
- You may tell her there's nothing to worry about, but she'll just think you can't understand how she feels.
- You may promise to come home early to provide her with some relief, but she'll only feel guilty as a result.
- You can tell her how great a mother she is, but she'll just think you're saying it so that she'll feel better.

What you can say instead, though, is:
- That things really will get better.
- That you understand she's feeling terrible.
- That she's taking all the right steps to feel better.
- That mistakes are okay; no one is perfect.
- That she's working hard.
- Tell her you love her.

*Don't* say:

- Get over it.
- That you're tired of her being like this.
- That this is the happiest period of her life.
- That you liked her better before.
- That she'll snap out of it.
- That it's just a phase.
- That all mothers experience this.
- That she should change her hair, lose weight, or buy new clothes.
- That she'll feel better if she took more time off work, or goes back to work, or got out more, or stayed in more.

There are plenty of practical things that you can do around the house to help your wife if she's feeling down.

- Pick up extra chores.
- Take care of dinner, or order in.
- Attend her doctor's appointments with her.
- If she has PPD (Postpartum depression), educate yourself on it.
- Make a list of the outlets she has to turn to when she really needs a break.
- Be with her. It's the simplest and most effective method. Take five minutes to just be with her, no other distractions, and let her know you're right beside her all the way.

You can also try the following:

- Make eye contact during conversations.

- Call her to see how her day is going. If she's having a particularly bad day, give her an extra call.
- Encourage her to nap whenever possible.
- Take over so that she can enjoy uninterrupted sleep.
- Listen, and be patient.

Remember:
- There may be things she used to love that only exhaust her, or feel like too much effort right now.
- You may think something will make her feel better, but that doesn't mean it will work.
- Any important decisions should be postponed until she's feeling better.
- If a decision cannot wait, then make it together.
- There are particular decisions, such as work, childcare, and breastfeeding, that will seem enormous. You can help her through those decisions by talking them through together, and analyzing the pros and cons.

If you can afford home help to come and take care of the cleaning once a week, that would relieve a heavy burden from your wife's shoulders.

It's incredibly important that she has time for herself, as well as time with you. It's important for you to have time on your own, too. So, come up with a schedule that allows you both to have some private time, and enlist the help of family or friends to babysit for you to enjoy a date night together. At the very least, you should make time to enjoy one date together every month.

# HARD DAYS

It doesn't matter who you are; parenting is stressful. Whether you're rich or poor, both parents work, there's a stay at home parent, or you're a single parent. It can be difficult to handle just one child while remaining calm, cool, and collected. It can be even more difficult to maintain your energy levels to get through the day. You should expect hard days as a parent, but there are plenty of ways you can manage your stress, and help you handle even the worst eventualities. The following tips can apply to both parents, whether you're at work all day, or at home with the kids:

- Get up just a bit earlier so that any mishaps will feel less stressful.
- Get everything ready the night before, from lunches, and outfits, to setting the table for breakfast.
- Create a schedule to remind you of *everything*.
- Don't procrastinate.
- Always plan ahead.
- Don't accept something that isn't working properly.
- Limit caffeine.
- Always have a contingency plan.
- Don't chase perfection.
- Look for the silver lining.
- Just say no to extra activities and projects that you don't have the time for.
- Unplug. Take time to soak in a long bath, take a nap, read in quiet, meditate, or practice yoga.

- Focus on needs, and forget about preferences. You *need* to eat, you need to drink water, you need clean clothes, and to stay warm (or cool). Everything else is just a preference, let it go.
- Learn deep breathing so that even when you're experiencing stress, you can manage it effectively.
- Make time for each other and talk out your worries and problems.
- Keep a journal to process your thoughts and feelings.
- Live a day at a time.
- Do something that you really enjoy every single day.
- Forget negative self-talk, and work on positive affirmations.
- Don't try to multitask, no matter how tempting it is. Focus on just getting one thing at a time.
- Make time for a bit of quiet and privacy every day.
- Don't get hung up on counting to 10, count however high you need to if it stops you from doing or saying something you shouldn't.
- Take advantage of weekends. It should be a change of pace.
- Don't do anything you'll need to lie about later.

The behavior of our children isn't always the core reason of parenting stress, though it may always feel like it. We get stressed out because we adore our kids, and we're determined to make their lives great. It's only natural that things will get difficult when you combine that stress with everything else going on in life.

The things that generally upset us the most are hot button issues, things that were established in our own childhoods. For instance, if you grew up in a strict family with shouting and roughhousing, you may get stressed out about physical play.

It may be stressful for you to watch your child play freely and romp through the house, but you can't allow this trigger to trap you. If you accept that issues from your childhood cause you to react or feel badly as a parent, then you've taken an important step. You can stop blaming yourself for reacting, and you can stop blaming your kids for how you feel.

You have now taken control over your own emotions, because now, you can determine:

- What events from your childhood cause you stress.
- What triggers are present in your current life.
- How you react to stress, and how to change these reactions so they don't rub off on your kids.

There are just three basic ways to tackle hard days:

- Shift your mind from the bad feelings that triggered your emotions.
- Let go of the feelings that are bubbling up.
- Stop the trigger before it has a chance to build up.

There are a number of ways to practice each strategy, consider the following:

**Shift Your Mind**

- **Change the scene.** If you find yourself losing control, it's time to change the scenery. You can take the kids for a walk, or get them out of the car, run a bath, or stop the activity that's causing your stress to build. If you need to cry, let it out.

- **Cuddle.** Everyone gets frustrated with their children. Even if you're feeling upset by their behavior, a cuddle break can help. Just feeling their warmth, skin, and the curl of their ringlets can be enough to break the stress that's taking over both of you.

- **Lie down.** Kids can be stubborn, and they often get locked in the habit of opposing us at every twist and turn. Our response is to control every minute of their behavior. When you notice this, take a time out and lie down on the floor. There's no need to offer any explanations. This can alter the power balance that has been working against you. You'll take your kids by surprise, and they'll find a way to make contact and reconnect with you.

**Let Go**

- **Call a friend.** Just hearing a friendly voice can be enough to help you work out your feelings.

- **Let go.** Our kids go through *multiple* stress episodes every day. They let their feelings out by having a tantrum and then laughing. The best way to handle this is by offering your child attentive support while they go through their meltdown. It will help them process their feelings quicker. The problem, in their mind, will be resolved and they'll feel closer to you.

- **Show your feelings.** We expend a lot of energy trying to keep our emotions in. That rubs off on the kids, so let your kids see you show your feelings, even if it means crying in front of them. That doesn't mean you need to *tell* them about the problem, you can simply tell them you're letting your feelings out.

**Stop the Trigger**

This requires planning, and you can even involve the kids in it. If you know there's a time of day that situations drive you to the edge, plan how you'll control it.

- **Special time.** This is great whether you have one kid or three. Dedicate special time for one on one play with your child. It's a special bonding time, and it can make a massive difference in their behavior. You can set the timer, and agree to play whatever game or activity your child chooses. Let your kid be in charge and just have fun. This is a great way to diffuse the power struggles that tends to dominate family life.
- **Regular breaks.** Parents need breaks, so find time to unwind and let go of all the stress. Whether it's during naptime, or before they wake up.

Remember, no matter how bad a day you're having, or how stressed you are, you're still a good parent.

Listen to this song whenever you are feeling down.

**Chris Tomlin - Good Good Father**

https://youtu.be/CqybaIesbuA

*This is a QR code that can be read by e.g.: NeoReader, a smartphone application. This QR code is the same YouTube link you see above.*

# WORK-LIFE BALANCE

Wake up early to get the kids ready for preschool, or school, drop them off, get to work, finish work, pick the kids up, ferry them to their after-school activities... then once you are home, there's homework and dinner to make, before getting the kids to bed. Welcome to your new life, because this will be happening 5 days a week, every week (minus summer) for the next forever, well, until they have their driver's licenses.

This truly is the grind, and a bittersweet one at that. This is the juggling act that every working parent deals with. If you want to survive the grind with your sanity intact, then there's something you need to let go of: perfection. Even the Harlem Globetrotters lost (like 6 times in almost 100 years). So, expect to take some L's, but it's okay, trust me. There will be times that you arrive late to activities, or maybe even not at all. Don't be ashamed of yourself when these issues crop up. Know that you are still a good parent, and you're doing the best job possible at keeping everything together.

Keeping it together isn't easy, my friend. There's a lot of preparation involved with just getting by! There will be times when you have to change plans, because your kids have failed to alert you to an important event, or waited till the night before a project is due to bring it up. There are ways to prevent this from happening, though, like planning your meals in advance, charting chores, and even creating a family calendar to include all activities, school projects, and any other scheduled events. The best part, you can even schedule in some R&R.

There's a lot of stress in just working full-time, so add the demands of parenthood on top of that, and it's no wonder it takes a toll. The majority of employees find that the demands of their job interfering with personal responsibilities, and almost the same say the reverse. Sometimes it seems as though there aren't enough hours available to meet everyone's needs.

You may feel guilty about trying to balance your work life with your home life, and trying to get some time on your own. Don't. You're already making plenty of sacrifices for your family. You'll face the temptation to stay late at work to avoid the battles at home. You'll consider bringing work home, only to upset the balance at home. It's all about balance.

I make sacrifices in a bid to maintain a happy work-life balance:

**Pride**

You know that saying about it taking a village to raise a child? There's nothing wrong with asking for help. You may have to swallow your pride and chirp up to ask, but asking for help is the key to success! You don't have to *depend* on others, but you'll become adept at trading favors. Like, setting up a carpool that will get the kids to and from school so that you have time off from that drive. Or, volunteering to deal with all the soccer activities one weekend, so that you get a reprieve the next. With a weekend that actually feels like a weekend, you'll be recharged for the work week ahead.

**Misconceptions**

You don't always have to split your time equally to be successful. There will be times when the balance tilts for the family, and other times when the work balance takes precedence. Successful parents sacrifice the belief that they need to divide their time equally, and instead, stay flexible. If you start to feel the balance is tilting the wrong direction, you can make some adjustments.

**Self-Neglect**

A great way to explain this is the emergency procedures you follow when flying. When the oxygen masks drop, you're supposed to put your mask on before you assist anyone else, *even* your children. When you're overwhelmed and exhausted, workout seems impossible and selfish. The cold hard fact of it, though, is that those are the exact times where you need that time the most.

Every successful parent knows that self-care will make you more productive and more efficient in the long-run. Sleep, relaxation, healthy diet, and exercise are now more important than ever. The good news is you'll stay fairly active chasing those rugrats around.

**Desires**

Every parent wants happy children, but here's the thing: Parents who strike successful balance between work and home life don't live and breathe just to make their children happy. Their goal is to raise confident, responsible children who will become equally confident and responsible as adults. They give their kids chores, teaching them responsibility without yelling, or nagging. They create clear consequences, and they aren't afraid to follow through on them. They role model the way and understand that children will face disappointment.

**Guilt**

You will feel guilty about working. Let's be honest, there are a *lot* of parents who would rather not be working full-time. The fact is that it isn't an option for many families. Whether both parents work full-time, or there's a balance, not many families can afford for a parent to stay home. Successful parents let go of the guilt they may feel about working. That guilt is wasted energy, which you could be using to find a solution. Perhaps you can arrange flexible hours, or learn to accept that it's a necessity.

If you want to strike a successful work-life balance, then you need to understand that sometimes working hard to meet your kid's needs is making them your priority, even if it doesn't feel like it. You have bills to pay, and working is the way to do it. Just because you're a working parent doesn't mean that you can't be a great parent. Successful parents will focus all of their spare time and excess energy raising their children, rather than wishing they didn't have to go to work.

# BE THERE

When it's time to send your child to preschool it may feel like it's harder for you, but remember, your child is also beginning a new stage of learning. Of course, you're going to feel anxious about the transition, or even concerned about whether you've chosen the right school or not. You will probably wonder what you can do to encourage a love of learning that will stick with them through school and beyond.

Our understanding of how children learn seems to change constantly. Though, the most recent consensus is that their emotional and social health will play a vital role in their academic success. Children who learn emotional and social skills in their preschool years are far less likely to experience behavioral issues through school. Less behavioral issues mean that there will be fewer obstacles between them and learning. There is a wide range of ways you can provide your child with emotional support to ensure they get the best from their learning experience, building a strong foundation for their future.

**Inspire Learning**

- **Ask about their day.** This will allow your child to recall what was learned, share it and build on it, all while building his self-esteem and confidence. Make sure you ask specific questions. If your child isn't forthcoming, ask specific questions about what they did at a particular time, or what story they heard.
- **Be patient.** As your child starts to learn new skills, don't pressure them. Let your child set the pace. If you allow your child to be

independent in the home, then they will carry that confidence into school.

- **Celebrate effort.** Put art projects and work on display. Don't tell them they're talented or that they're smart, offer meaningful praise. Focus on the process rather than the result, talk about how they were patient during a difficult step, or ask why they chose particular colors.

- **Listen.** You may be busy watching television or reading a book, but if your child has something to share with you, you need to offer them attention and listen. You need to show them that you respect their thoughts and feelings, because this will boost their confidence, and encourage them to keep talking, even as they get older.

- **Encourage questioning.** I know that being asked a million questions is exhausting. Especially when it's what or why in response to everything you say. However, when you respond to their natural curiosity, it encourages them to continue asking questions as they pursue their interests in life.

- **Show your pride.** The encouragement your child gets from seeing your face light up when they make something new, or take on a new challenge, is incomparable.

- **Let them teach you.** If you've ever trained someone, or successfully explained a concept to someone, then you'll know that teaching others reinforces your knowledge. Kids love this roleplay, and by allowing them to teach you, you're providing them with confidence. It also provides you with the opportunity to find out what your child has been learning.

- **Allow them space.** You might be able to do it faster, but *don't*. Allow them the space to learn how to do things for themselves, and help if they ask for it. Don't point out mistakes unless your child asks. For instance, if they're trying to find all of the hidden objects in a puzzle.

- **Support their learning style.** Everyone learns differently, some people learn better by doing, some by hearing, and some by seeing. Understand how your child learns, and support their learning style.

## Be Engaged with Their Schooling

- **Support them with difficulties.** If your child is struggling with school, don't play the blame game. This will create shame, which can cause lasting psychological damage. Your child is trying their best.

- **Get involved.** You should make an effort to get to know teachers and members of the faculty. They'll know what challenges your child has. If you have the time to get involved, then volunteer for field trips and school projects. There may be opportunities for you to help, even if you work full-time.

## Create a Supportive Environment

- **Play is important.** It's important at home and in school. Think of play as the job of children; it's their work in early childhood. Play is how a child practices skills, learns to solve problems, as well as organize thinking. Make sure that your child has free time to explore these challenges in unstructured play.

- **Establish routines, rules, and structure.** Better behavior comes as a result of predictability and consistency. Be consistent when it comes to meals, bedtime, and other activities. When your child is still in preschool, help them master brushing their teeth, getting dressed, and preparing for school. Establish clear family rules, such as always brush your teeth before bed, no biting, no hitting, no scratching, etc.

- **Identify your values.** What's important to your family? Aside from academics. Ensure that you are clear about your values and expectations. Your actions and words should reinforce these. If you want your child to practice kindness, then be kind and praise their kindness as an achievement.

- **Show empathy.** At the root of childhood issues is a lack of empathy. For instance, bullying, cheating, depression, and anxiety. Kids who can share and help others in kindergarten are much more likely to achieve success in later life. So, teach empathy.

- **Limit their screen time.** Excessive screen time results in lower grades. So, be careful about how much time they spend in front of the screen, because this detracts from time that could be spent reading, playing, and interacting. I'm not saying it should be zero because nowadays we are checking Facebook on our smartphones, surfing the web on our tablets, and do online shopping or basically anything. This is completely different compared to the time when we were children. I'm just saying you should allocate time for other activities as well for your child's and for your own sake.

- **Encourage experimentation.** You may roll your eyes and worry about the mess of an impending magic potion, but allow them to express their creativity and curiosity. Even if the fridge door has been open for 5 minutes while they find potion ingredients.

- **Positive alternatives.** Making mistakes is part of learning, and trial and error help to build knowledge. Rather than correcting mistakes, encourage your child to try, try, and try again, and when they get it right - cheer them on.

# BOND OF TRUST

What is Trust between you and your child? As you continuously speak with your child honestly and respectfully, the Trust and bond between you will grow.

Imagine that you are playing a good MMORPG, like WoW. Ah, those all-night-long raids in Naxxramas and Ulduar. I miss my hunter so much.

Let's say, there are six Levels of Trust in your relationship:
- 0/ Careful
- 1/ Reliable
- 2/ Trustful
- 3/ Friendly
- 4/ Loyal
- 5/ Symbiotic

With a higher level of trust, your adult child will more likely to call you when she will have news to share or need advice from somebody wise and respected.

Make them feel and understand that you can always count on each other to tell the truth. *Always.* It has to be the backbone of your family. If they are angry, desperate or sad, they should not be ashamed of talking about it at home. Do you remember? You.are.their.safety.net.

You can't expect them to tell you the truth if you're not honest with them. Be brief and be age appropriate in your response if needed. Of course, all of us have a right to a private life, and you need to draw careful boundaries when sharing things which they are not ready for. Like politics. I'm not sure if I'm already ready for that BS. Your goal should be to create a homely environment where there are no secrets, and everyone feels comfortable being truthful.

Don't forget that they might not be perfect truth-tellers every time. Fortunately, perfection isn't one of our goals.

For a trusting relationship to develop, there must be consistency in your relationship. The more often each of you demonstrates that you can be trusted, the more likely you will be trusted. Consistency strengthens every relationship.

I almost forgot good reflexes. That also helps in strengthening the trust. Check the video.

**17 Incredible Moments When Dad Saved the Day**
https://youtu.be/qoQssWPRNR0

*This is a QR code that can be read by e.g.: NeoReader, a smartphone application. This QR code is the same YouTube link you see above.*

# Quotes About Fatherhood

I have collected a few motivating quotes, poems, and thoughts to help myself gain extra energy. Let me share them with you hoping that you will use them whenever you need their help.

*"My father gave me the greatest gift anyone could give another person, he believed in me."*

– Jim Valvano

*"My father was my teacher. But most importantly he was a great dad."*

– Beau Bridges

*"A real man loves his wife, and places his family as the most important thing in life. Nothing has brought me more peace and content in life than simply being a good husband and father."*

– Frank Abagnale

*"I cannot think of any need in childhood as strong as the need for a father's protection."*

– Sigmund Freud

*"Anyone can be a father, but it takes someone special to be a dad, and that's why I call you dad, because you are so special to me. You taught me the game and you taught me how to play it right."*

– Wade Boggs

*"I hope I am remembered by my children as a good father."*

– Orson Scott Card

*"It is easier for a father to have children than for children to have a real father."*

– Pope John XXIII

*"The greatest thing a FATHER can do to his children, is to love their mother."*

– Anjaneth Garcia Untalan

*"I've had a hard life, but my hardships are nothing against the hardships that my father went through in order to get me to where I started."*

– Bartrand Hubbard

*"A dad is someone who
wants to catch you before you fall
but instead picks you up,
brushes you off,
and lets you try again.*

*A dad is someone who
wants to keep you from making mistakes
but instead lets you find your own way,
even though his heart breaks in silence
when you get hurt.*

*A dad is someone who*
*holds you when you cry,*
*scolds you when you break the rules,*
*shines with pride when you succeed,*
*and has faith in you even when you fail...."*

– Unknown

# BE TRUE TO YOURSELF

Every parent will experience self-loss while they're parenting. *Yes*, having a child changes everything, and *yes, it is* life changing, because you are now responsible for the well-being of another human being. Your life will be turned upside down, shaken, and changed.

Is there any need to lose yourself just to be a good parent?

Take a look at traditional cultures. In Africa, children are an asset; it's simply a continuation of life, there is no need to lose who you are as a result. The difference in Africa is that parents are parenting within a community, rather than beside it like in the western world. There are closer family ties, and parents often have their children with them all the time.

We've lost that, and we've replaced it with something different:

Child-centeredness. Since we can't spend our every moment with our children, we make the most of the time we do have. We sit with them, play, and read them stories. This is obviously natural, and healthy, but we cater to every whim of our children's wants, desires, and needs. Kids thrive with active parents; they can tend to themselves and function without having their parent at their side constantly.

How can you parent and be true to yourself?

- Provide a safe environment for your child to explore and roam free.

- Trust your child, there's no need to fret and hover.

- Be active, and follow your passions.

- Don't make room in your life for your child; it should be the other way round.

- Build a community of care around you.

- Having kids shouldn't prevent you from doing anything. It will just require additional planning and sound judgement.

I won't lie, I had a debate with myself on whether to include this chapter or not. It can be a controversial topic. The truth is, though, many parents feel like this when they have children. You're not alone, and being true to yourself shouldn't be a source of guilt.

Whether you are a working parent, or you stay at home, you will experience this loss of self. You get so caught up in the task at hand that you forget who *you* are. You start to fit in with the people around you, and take on tasks that you normally wouldn't be interested in. Suddenly you realize you've turned into something you're not.

So, what does it mean to be you?

- **Being a hands-on dad.** This is part of you who you are now, so be true to yourself by embracing it.

- **Dressing like yourself.** Becoming a dad doesn't mean you have to drop t-shirts for button downs or board shorts for khakis. If your style happens to be khakis, that's cool too. Your wardrobe is an expression of your personality, and of who you are. You may get caught up trying to emulate those around you; you think that because you're a dad you should dress or behave a certain way. You don't need to change who you are to be a better dad.

- **Back to Basics.** Whether it's nature that you love, the outdoors in general, the beach, baseball games, or *whatever*. You can still do all of this and include your children. Introduce your kids to the things that you love and make family traditions.

- **To Do List.** A great way to get back to who you are is by creating a to-do list. This one may sound farfetched, but it's true. Everyone creates lists, but they tend to become complex, almost breathing beings. They're a complex balance of musts, haves, wishes, and wants, and rarely do these lists include having fun on your own, or even having a good time with your children. So, take the time to prioritize your lists. Sometimes you need to forget about the yard work and just do something for yourself. Your focus shouldn't just be on the musts and haves.

- **The Rhythm.** Everyone has a flow to their time and their days. Schedules are great, but sometimes you have to enjoy a twist and turn.

- **Say No.** While the world around you demands a yes for everything, you need to learn to say no. Sometimes you just don't have the energy or the time to say yes to everything. Why do you always say yes? Because you don't want to let people down. Forget about letting others down, worry about letting yourself down.

- **Make time.** Do you love playing the guitar, playing video games, the beach, or swimming? You don't have to say goodbye to those things, you just have to make time for them. Guess what? Kids will play video games for hours, just hand them a broken controller and plop them in your lap. The real key to being true to yourself is showing your children what you're passionate about. It's important for them to see you as a person, and not just as a parent. It's important that you show them what true passion is, and it's equally as important for them to see that you are important. That you do things with love, and with passion.

Life has changed, but you don't need to sacrifice who you are to be a great parent. This is what I need to do to be true to myself, to rediscover the man that I am, the me I want to be, and the parent I need to be.

What do you need to do to remain true to yourself? Can you be true to yourself through parenthood?

You're as ready as you'll ever be, and any time you start to worry about whether you'll be a good dad or a good partner... you can circle back to this book for a reminder that you're doing your best.

*Your Friend,*
*George*

P.S.: Be.there.for.them.

*Could I ask you a favour? If you did enjoy this book, could leave me a review on Amazon? If you search for my name and the title on Amazon you will find it. Thank you so much, it is very much appreciated!*

*Feel free to join my Facebook group (Self-Confidence Boom) for frequent blog posts and motivational quotes as part of this book's offering: https://www.facebook.com/selfconfidenceboom*

# REFERENCES

- http://bmjopen.bmj.com/content/6/11/e012034
- http://brainyquote.com
- http://boardofwisdom.com

Made in the USA
Monee, IL
22 July 2021

74112337R00049